Business Arabic

Business Arabic

An Essential Vocabulary

John Mace

Edinburgh University Press

© John Mace, 2008

Edinburgh University Press Ltd
22 George Square, Edinburgh

Typeset in Times, Helvetica and Giza and printed and bound
in Great Britain by Antony Rowe Ltd, Chippenham, Wilts

A CIP record for this book is available from the
British Library

ISBN 978 0 7486 3339 5 (paperback)

CONTENTS

INTRODUCTION

This book aims to help students of Arabic, whether at university or in the workplace, to handle confidently the Arabic vocabulary used in business. It can be used either as support for a work-oriented Arabic course, or as an extension of general Arabic studies.

The entries are listed in Arabic alphabetical order within each of the ten chapters. Words usually accompanied by the article are shown with the article, but in the alphabetical position of the word itself. Compound expressions occupy the position of their most significant Arabic word. The English equivalents of all entries are also listed alphabetically in the Index.

Chapter 1 lists terms of general use and specialised terms for which there is no chapter in the book. Wherever appropriate, specialised terms are listed for preference in Chapters 2 to 10. The same word may also appear with different meanings or uses in different chapters. The Index can also help your search.

Nouns, adjectives, verbs and adverbs are pointed with only those vowels which are not clear from the spelling or grammar. Also pointed are one-letter words ـب , ل and و when shown prefixed. Other words are unpointed. و , ا , أ and ي represent 'a or a', ā, ū and ī respectively unless the pointing, spelling or grammar indicate otherwise. Further:

- *Nouns and adjectives* are shown as follows:
  Gender: only where unclear from spelling or meaning.
  Isolated adjectives are shown in the masculine singular.
  Pointing: without case-endings, without *shadda* on the masculine *nisba* ending, but with final ى \ ـِ ... on

indefinite masculine weak nouns and adjectives.

Plural: only where broken; where none is shown it is sound (ون... -*ūn* or ات... -*āt*). Plurals are not shown in compound expressions.

• *Verbs* are shown as follows:

Form I triliteral: first principal part (i.e. past tense), the government if this differs from the English, and the verbal noun (مصدر); the notation I, and the variable vowel of the second principal part (i.e. present tense).

Forms II-X triliteral: first principal part (unpointed except for ... *shadda*), the government if this differs from the English, and the notation II to X.

Quadriliteral: as for II-X triliteral, but with notation IQ or IIQ and the verbal noun for Form IQ.

Participles, Verbal noun: listed separately only in cases of special importance, meaning or difficulty.

• *Construct expressions* (إضافات) are shown in the definite form where this is more common.

Abbreviations and symbols in the vocabulary indicate:

adj.	adjective	pl.	plural
cst.	construct	Q	quadriliteral
e.o.	each other	s.o.	someone
f.	feminine	s.t.	something
I-X	verb form	ه	direct person-object
int.	intransitive	ـه	direct thing-object
m.	masculine	+	and
n.	noun	\ , /	or

I am greatly indebted to Kifah Hanna for her valuable revision and improvement of this text, and to Marilyn Moore for her tireless proofreading.

1. GENERAL

اِبْتِداءً مِن	with effect from
اِبْتِدائي	initial, preliminary
اتِّجاه	trend
اتِّحاد	union, association
الاتِّحاد الأُوروبيّ	European Union
اتِّخاذ القَرارات	decision-making (n.)
اتِّفاقيّة	agreement
اتّفق مع على	VIII to agree with s.o. on s.t.
إجْراء	procedure, measure
أجّل	II to postpone/defer
إجْمالي	gross, total (adj.)
احْتِكار	monopoly
احْتِياطي	reserve (n.)
عِلْم الإحْصاء :إحصاء	statistics
إحْصائي	statistical, statistician
إحْصائيّات	statistics
اخْتِيار	choice
أدار هـ	IV to manage/direct
إدارة	management, administration
إدارة بالأهْداف	management by objectives

الأَدْنى	minimum
أَرجأَ	IV to postpone/defer
اِزداد int	VIII to increase
أَزْمة أَزَمات	crisis
أَساس أُسُس	basis
دِراسة :أَساليب الأَساليب	methods study
اِسْتْراتيجيّة	strategy
اِستشار	X to consult
اِسْتِشاري	advisory
اِسْتِقْرار	stability
استهلك	X to consume
أسّس	II to establish/found/ incorporate
أُسْلوب أَساليب	method, system, technique
اشترك ·	VIII to participate/cooperate
أشرف على	IV to supervise
أشْغال (عُموميّة\ مَدَنيّة)	(public/civil) works
أخَذَ بعَيْن :اعتبار الاعْتِبار	to take into consideration
اِعْتَبارًا ل	in view of

اِعْتَبارًا من	with effect from
اعتبر	VIII to consider
أعْمال .pl	business
أغْلَبيّة	majority
افتتح	VIII to inaugurate
الأقْصى	maximum
إقْليم أَقاليم	region
أقَلّية	minority
أكْثَريّة	majority
أكَّد	II to confirm, to substantiate
أكيد	certain, sure (of things), certainly
ألْغى	IV to cancel
الشَرِكة الأُمّ أَمّ:	parent company
أمان	security
اِمْتِياز	concession, franchise
أمْر أُمور	affair, matter
أمَّم	II to nationalise
أمْن	security
أمين عامّ	secretary-general
اِنْتِعاش	boom
انتَهِز (فُرْصةً)	VIII to seize (an opportunity)

أنجز	IV to implement
انحرف (عن)	VII to deviate (from)
انخفض int.	VII to decrease/be reduced
أنشأ	IV to organise
انْفِرادي	unilateral
انهار	VII to collapse/crash
أهْلي	domestic
أوْلَويّة	priority
إيجابي	positive
بَحَثَ هـ\عن بَحْث بُحوث	I *a* to search for/look into
بَراءة اخْتِراع	patent
بَرْنامَج بَرامِج	programme
بَضاعة بَضائِع	ware, goods, merchandise
بَقيّة بَقايا	remainder
بَلَغَ هـ بُلوغ	I *u* to amount to
بيروقْراطيّة	bureaucracy
بيئة	environment
تاجِر تُجّار	trader, merchant, dealer
تأخّر	V to be delayed
تأْييدًا ل	in support of
تِجاري	trading/commercial/

business (adj.)

تَجْريبي pilot/test (adj.)

تَحْديد حُرّيّة التَصَرُّف restrictive practice

تَحْقيق investigation

تخصّص V to specialise

تَدْبير تَدابير arrangement, measure

تَدَرُّج وَظيفي chain of command

تركّز في int. V to concentrate on

تَسَلْسُل sequence, succession

تَشْغيل operating (n.), operation

تطوّر int. V to develop/evolve

تعاوُنيّة cooperative (n.)

تعرف: الاتِّفاقيّة العامّة General Agreement on Tariffs
لالتَعْريفات الجُمْرُكيّة and Trade (GATT)
والتجارة
(الجات\الجات)

تَفْضيل preference

تَفْويض السُلْطة delegation of authority

تقدّم int. V to progress/advance

تَقْدير تَقادير evaluation

تَقْرير decision

تَقْرير تَقارير report

تِكْنولوجيا	technology
تَمْهيدي	preparatory, provisional, exploratory
تَنْظيم	(act of) organising, organisation
التَنْظيم وَطُرُق العَمَل	organisation and methods (OM)
تَنْفيذ	implementation
تَنْفيذي	executive (adj.)
تَنْمِيَة	development
تَوْجيه	orientation
توسّع int.	V to expand
توقّع	V to expect, to anticipate
ثقة (في)	trust, confidence (in)
ثُلاثي الأطْراف	trilateral, tripartite
ثُنائي	bilateral
جارٍ (الجاري)	ongoing
جامِعة الدُوَل العَرَبيّة	League of Arab States
جدّد هـ	II to modernise/renew
جُزْئي	partial
جَماعي	group (adj.)
جهة: مِن جِهَتَيْن	bilateral(ly)
جهة: مِن جِهة واحِدة	unilateral(ly)
حافِز حَوافِز	incentive

حافظ على	III to preserve/maintain (practice/situation)
حالي	current (adj.)
حَدّ حُدود	limit, margin
حَدّي	marginal
حَصَلَ على حُصول	I *u* to attain/achieve
حقّق	II to implement
حقّق في	II to investigate
حَقْل حُقول	field, domain
حَقيقة حَقائِق	fact
حَلَّ هـ حَلّ حُلول	I *u* to solve, dissolve
حَلّ المُعْضِلات\ المَشاكِل	problem-solving (n.)
حِماية	protection (trade)
حوّل	II to transfer
خاصّ	private
خاصيّة خَصائِص	characteristic (n.)
خاطر بـ	III to risk
خِبْرة	experience, expertise
خَبير خُبَراء	expert
خَطأ أخْطاء	error
خُلُق أخْلاق	ethic

خِيار option

دافِع دَوافِع incentive

دائِرة دَوائِر department, directorate

دَائِم permanent

دبّر II to arrange/devise

دَرَجة grade, degree

دَمَجَ في دَمْج int I *u* to merge with

دَوْرة cycle

دَوْري periodic

دُوَلي international

رُبْع سَنَوي quarterly

رتّب II to arrange

رَجْعي retroactive, retrospective, reactionary

:رجعي بِتَأْثير رَجْعي with retroactive effect

:رجوع لا رُجوع فيه irrevocable

رخّص ل ب\في II to license/authorise

رُخْصة رُخَص licence, permit

رَسْمي official (adj.), formal

رَفَضَ رَفْض I *i/u* to refuse/reject

رَقْم أرْقام figure, number

ركّز هـ في II to concentrate s.t. on

رَمْزي	symbolic, token (adj.)
رَئيس رؤَساء	chairman, director
رَئيسي	principal, key (adj.)
رِئَاسة\رياسة	chairmanship, directorship
زادَ هـ\int. زيادة	I *ī* to increase
زوّد ب	II to supply
سابِقة	precedent, precedence
سَبَب أَسْباب	cause
سِفارة	embassy
سَفير سُفَراء	ambassador
سِكْرَتيرة	secretary
سَلْبي	negative
سِلْسِلة سَلاسِل	series
سُلْطة	authority
سِمْسار سَماسِرة	broker
سهّل هـ ل\على	II to facilitate
سِيَاحة	tourism
سِياسة	policy, politics
سَيْطر على	IQ to dominate
شَبَكة شِباك\sound	network
شَرْط شُروط	(pre-)condition
شَرِكة	company, corporation

شَريك شُرَكاء	partner
شُغْل أشْغال	work, occupation
شَغّل هـ	II to operate s.t.
شَهادة	certificate
شُهْرة	reputation
صافٍ (الصافي)	net(t)
صَحيح	correct, right (adj.)
بِصِفَتِه ...اً	in his capacity as …
صَفْقة صَفَقات	transaction
صِفة	quality, attribute, characteristic
صَمّم	II to design
صِناعة	industry
ضَبَطَ ضَبْط	I *u/i* to check, to control
ضَرورة	necessity
طارِئ طَوارِئ	contingency, emergency
طبّق هـ على	II to apply s.t. to
طَبيعي	natural, normal
طوّر هـ	II to develop
عاجِل	urgent
عالَمي	world (adj.)
عامّ	public, general
عامِل عَوامِل	factor (thing)

عجّل II to expedite

عُرْف practice (established custom)

عُضْو أعْضاء member

عُضْوِيّة membership

عُطْلة عُطَل holiday

عَلاقة relation(ship)

عَمِلَ (هـ) عَمَل أعْمال I a to do, to work, to make

عَمَل أعْمال work, labour

عَمَلي practical

عَهِدَ إلى بِ I a to entrust to s.o. s.t.

غُرْفة التِجارة chamber of commerce

فاقَ فَوْق I ū to exceed

فَتْرة فَتَرات period

فتّش هـ II to inspect

فَحَصَ فَحْص فُحوص I a to examine/test

فُرْصة فُرَص chance, opportunity

فَرْع فُروع branch

فَشِلَ فَشَل I a to fail

فَصَلَ من\بين فَصْل I i to separate

فضّل II to prefer

فَعّال effective, efficient

فَعّالِيّة effectiveness, efficiency

فَنّي	technical
فوّض هـ إلى\ل	II to delegate
قائمة سَوْداء	black list
قَبِلَ ه هـ قَبول	I *a* to accept
قُدْرة (على)	capacity (to/for)
قَرار	decision
قرّر	II to decide
قِسْم أقْسام	division, department
قَصْد	purpose
قِطاع	sector
قَوْمي	national
كامِل	complete
كَفالة	sponsorship
كَفيل كُفَلاء	sponsor
كَمّيّة	quantity
لَجْنة لِجان	committee, commission, board
لوّث	II to pollute
مالِك مُلّاك	owner
مُباشِر	direct (adj.), immediate
مَبْدأ مَبادئ	principle
مُتَأكِّد	certain, sure, convinced
مُتَخَصِّص	specialist, specialised

مُتَسَلْسِل serial

مُتَعَدِّد الأطْراف multilateral

مُتَعَدِّد الجِنْسِيات multinational

مُتَغَيِّر variable (n./adj.)

مُتَنَوِّع miscellaneous

مُتَوازِن balanced

مُتَوَسِّط average/mean (n./adj.),

medium (adj.)

مَثَّل II to represent

مَجال field, domain

مَجْلِس الإدارة board of directors

مَجْموعة مَجاميع\ group

sound

مُحْتَمَل probable, potential (adj.)

محدد: لِغَرَض مُحَدَّد ad hoc

مَحْدود limited

مَحَلِّي local, domestic

مُخاطَرة risk

مُخَطَّط تَنْظيمي organigramme

مُدّة مُدَد period

على مُدّة ثابِتة fixed-term

على مُدّة مُتَوَسِّطة medium-term

على مُدّة مُحَدَّدة\ مَحْدودة	limited-term
مَدَني	civil
على مَدى طَويل	long-term
على مَدى قَصير	short-term
مُدير مُدَراء	manager, director
مُدير عامّ	general manager, director-general
مُرْجأ	deferred
مِرْحَلة مَراحِل	phase
مَرْكَز مَراكِز	centre
مَرْكَزي	central, centralised
مَرِن	flexible
مُرونة	flexibility, elasticity
مَسْألة مَسائِل	matter
مُستَشار	consultant
مُسْتَوىً (المُسْتَوى)	level (n.)
مَسَحَ مَسْح	I a to survey
مَسْؤوليّة مَحْدودة	limited liability
مُشاركة	partnership
مُشْتَرَك	joint, common
مَشْروط	conditional, qualified

مَشْروع مَشاريع project

مُشْكلة مَشاكِل problem

مَصْدَر مَصادِر source, resource

مَصْلَحة مَصالِح interest, concern

... مُضادّ opposing, counter-

(bid, proposal etc.)

مُعْضِلة problem

مِعْيَار مَعايِير criterion, norm, standard

مَقْبول acceptable

مُقيم resident

مَكان أمْكِنة\أماكِن place

مكتب مكاتب office

مَكْتَبي clerical

مُلْزِم binding

مِلْكي proprietary

مُناسِب appropriate, opportune

مُناسَبة opportunity, occasion

مُنافِس competitor

مُنافَسة competition

أعلن عن : مناقصة IV to call for tenders
مُناقَصة

مَنَحَ ه هـ مَنْح I a to grant

مُنْشَآت	premises, installations
مَنْصِب مَناصِب	office, post, function
مَنْطِق	logic, rationale
مِنْطَقة مَناطِق	area, region
مِنْطَقة صِناعيّة	industrial estate
مُنَظَّمة	organisation (body)
مُنْفَصِل	separate
مُنَوَّع	miscellaneous
مَهَمّة مَهامّ	task, assignment
مُوافَقة	agreement, consent
مَوْجود	available
مُؤَسَّسة	foundation, institution, enterprise
مُوَظَّف مَدَني\حُكومي	civil servant
مَوْرِد مَوارِد	resource
مُوَرِّد	supplier
مَوْعِد مَواعيد\مَواعِد	appointment (agreed date/time)
مَوْعِد أخير	deadline
مُوَقَّت\مُؤَقَّت	temporary, provisional
ميّز (بين وبين)	II to distinguish/discriminate/ differentiate (between)
نائِب نُوّاب	deputy

نائِب ...	deputy ..., vice-... (in cst.)
نَتيجة نَتائِج	result
نَجَحَ نَجاح	I *a* to succeed
نِزاع	conflict
نسّق	II to coordinate
نِظام أنْظِمة	system, regulation
نَظَري	theoretical
نَظَريّة	theory
نظّم	II to organise
نفّذ	II to execute/fulfil
مُنَظَّمة الدُوَل المُصَدِّرة للنَفْط (أوْبيك) :نفط	Organisation of Oil-Exporting Countries (OPEC)
نِقابة	syndicate
نَقَضَ هـ نَقْض	I *u* to revoke
بِلا نَقْض :نقض	irrevocable
نَقَصَ عن نَقْص	I *u* to fall short of
نُقْطة نُقَط	point
نُمُوّ	growth
نوّع هـ	II to diversify
نَوْعي	specific
نَوْعيّة	quality

نيّة نَوايا\sound	intention
حُسْن\سوء النيّة :نية	good/bad faith
هُبوط	slump, fall
هَدَف أهْداف	goal, target
هَيْكَل هَياكِل	structure
هَيْئة	board, commission
وافق (ه هـ\في\على)	III to agree (with s.o. on s.t.)
وجّه (هـ إلى\لـ)	II to direct (s.t. to)
وَحْدة	unit
وِزارة	ministry
وزّع	II to distribute, to allocate
وَزير وُزَراء	minister
وسّع هـ	II to expand
وَسيلة وَسائِل	means
وَطَني	national
وَظيفة وَظائِف	function
وِفاق	agreement, consent
وِقائي	protective (in trade), preventive
وَكالة	agency
وَكيل وُكَلاء	agent
ولّد	II to generate

2. DATA & COMMUNICATION

	اتِّصـال	communication
	اتَّصل ب	VIII to contact/telephone s.o.
	أتلف	IV to shred (paper)
أجاب هـ\إلى عن\على		IV to answer
جِهاز إجابة :إجابة		answering machine
	أدخل	IV to input/insert
	أرَّخ	II to date
	أرسل إلى\لـ هـ	IV to send/transmit
	استرجع	X to retrieve (data)
	استعلم (هـ) عن	X to enquire (of s.o.) about
	اسْتِلام	receipt (act)
وَصْل اسْتِلام :استلام		receipt (voucher)
	أُسْطُوانة	disk
	أشار إلى	IV to refer to
	إشارة	sign, reference
	أصدر هـ	IV to issue
	أعلن	IV to announce
	افْتِراضي	virtual
	ألحق	IV to attach/annex/append
	إلِكْتْرَوْني	electronic

إنْتِرْنِت	internet
أوجز هـ\في	IV to abridge/summarise
أوضح	IV to elucidate
إيصال	receipt (voucher)
بَرامِج .pl	software
برمج بَرْمَجة	IQ to program
بَرْنامَج بَرامِج	(computer, data) program
بَريد	mail
بَريد إلِكْتْرَوْني	e-mail
بِطاقة	card
بَيانات	data
تَحْليل	analysis
تَحْليلي	analytical
جِهاز تَصْوير تصوير:	(photo)copier
وَثايق	
تَعْليمات	instructions
تَغْذِيَة مُرْتَدّة\	feedback
اسْتِرْجائِيّة	
تَقْديم	presentation
آلة تَلّافة وَرَق تلاف:	(paper-)shredder
تنبّأ	V to forecast/project
جَدْوَل جَداوِل	schedule, table

جُمْلة جُمَل sentence

حاسِب computer

حَذَفَ حَذْف I *i* to delete

حرّر II to edit

حَفَظَ حِفْط I *a* to save (data)

حلّل II to analyse

خَتَمَ خَتْم أخْتام I *i* to seal

خَطّ خُطوط (telephone etc.) line/extension

خَطأ اخْطاء error

خطّط II to plan

خطّة خِطَط plan, scheme

دَخْل input

دِراسة study

دَعَمَ دَعْم I *a* to back up

:دفع وَحْدة دَفْع أقْراص disk drive

دَليل أدِلّة directory

دَمْغة stamp (impression)

ذَكَرَ ذِكْر I *u* to mention

راجع هـ III to review, to revert/refer to

راقب III to inspect/censor/check

رَدّاً على in reply to

رِسالة رَسائِل letter, note, message

	رَسْم رُسوم	drawing, graph, chart
	رقْمي	digital
	رَمْز رُموز	sign, symbol, code
	سجّل	II to register/record
	سرّ أسْرار	secret (n.)
	سرّي	secret (adj.), confidential
سلكي :	لا سلْكي	radio/wireless (adj.)
شارح:	رَسالة شارِحة	covering/explanatory letter
	شاشة	screen, monitor
	شَهادة	certificate
	صَفْحة صَفَحات	page, sheet
صلب:	قُرْص صُلْب	hard disk
	صنّف	II to classify/categorise/file
	طابع طَوابع	stamp (impression, paper)
طباعة:	(آلة) طباعة	printer
	طَبَعَ طَبْع	I *a* to print
	ظَرْف ظُروف	envelope
	عالج	III to process
	عبارة	expression, phrase
	عبّر عن	II to express
	عدّل	II to amend
	عَرض عُروض	display

عَلامة	label (computing)
عُنْوان عَناوِين	address
فاكُس	(tele)fax
فِهْرِس فَهارِس	index, table of contents
قُرْص أَقْراص	disk
قَناة قَنَوات	channel
آلة كاتِبة :كاتِب	typewriter
كَشَفَ هـ\عن كَشْف I i	to disclose
كَلِمة	word
كَمْبْيُوتَر	computer
لَوْحة أَلْواح\sound	(notice- etc.) board
مُبَيَّضة	fair copy
مَحْفوظات	archives
مُذَكِّرة	memorandum
مَذْكور (سابِقًا\آنِفًا)	(afore)mentioned
مُراسَلة	correspondence
مَرْجِع مَراجِع	reference (thing referred to)
قُرْص مَرِن :مرن	floppy disk
مُسْتَنَد	document
آلة مَسْح :مسح	scanner
مُسَوَّدة	draft, proof/rough copy
مُعالَجة المُعْطَيات\	data-processing

البَيانات	
مُعالَجة النُصوص	word-processing
مُعْطَيات	data
مَعْلومات .pl	information
مِلَفّ	file (of papers)
نِداء	paging
جِهاز نِداء :نِداء	beeper, paging device
نَسَخَ نَسْخ	I *a* to copy
نُسْخة نُسَخ (عن)	copy/duplicate (of)
نَشَرَ نَشْر	I *u* to publish
نَشْرة	bulletin, circular, publication
نَشْرة أخْبار	newsletter
نَصّ نُصوص	text
نَموذَج نَماذِج\sound	model, specimen (n.),
	form (document)
نَموذَجي	model, specimen (adj.)
وَثيقة وَثائِق	document
وَرَق collective	paper
وَرَقة أوْراق	paper
وقّع	II to (counter)sign

3. FINANCE

ائْتِمان	credit
أَجْر أُجور	fee, rate, pay, wage
إجْمالي الناتِج القَوْمي	gross national product (GNP)
إجْمالي الناتِج المَحَلّي	gross domestic product (GDP)
مَحْفَظة استثمار:	investment portfolio
مُسْتَنَدات	
الاسْتِثْمارات	
استثمر	X to invest
استردّ	X to recover (money)
استلم	VIII to receive
اعْتِماد	credit
اعْتِماد مالي	fund
أفلس	IV to be(come) bankrupt
اقترض	VIII to borrow
اقْتِصاد	economy, economics
إنْفاق	expenditure
إيراد	yield, return
بَنْك بُنوك	bank
البَنْك الدُوَلي	World Bank
بورْصة	stock exchange

تَضَخُّم	inflation
تَكْلِفة تَكاليف	cost
ثابِت	fixed (assets, prices)
ثَرْوَة	wealth
جمّد هـ	II to freeze
حامِل	bearer
حِساب	account, calculation
حِساب جارٍ (الجاري)	current account
حِساب وَدائِع	deposit account
حَوالة مَصْرِفيّة	banker's draft
حوّل	II to transfer
خَزينة خَزائِن	safe (n.), treasury
خَسِرَ هـ خَسارة خَسائِر	I *a* to lose
خصّص هـ لـ	II to appropriate (funds etc.) for
دائِن	creditor
دَخْل	income
دَفْتَر (حِساب)	(account) book, ledger
دَفَعَ (لـ\إلى هـ) دَفْع مَدْفوعات	I to pay
دَفْع مَدْفوعات	payment
دقّق	II to audit

دَيْن دُيون	debt
رَأْس مال	capital (n.)
رَأْسْمالي	capital (adj.), capitalist
رَبِحَ (مِن) رِبْح أَرْباح	I to profit (from)
رَسْم رُسوم	charge, fee
رَصيد أَرْصِدة	balance, available funds
سَحَبَ سَحْب	I a to withdraw (money)
سدّد	II to defray/amortise
سِعْر أَسْعار	price
سِعْر الصَرْف	exchange rate
سلّف ه هـ	II to advance
سَنَد	bond, security
سوّى هـ	II to settle (debt, dispute etc.)
سَهْم أَسْهُم	share
شيك	cheque
صَنْدوق النقْد الدُوَلي	International Monetary Fund (IMF)
ضَريبة ضَرائِب	tax
الضَريبة على القيمة المُضافة	value added tax (VAT)
ضَمان	bond, security, guarantee
عَجْز	deficit

عَدَد أعْداد	number
عدّل هـ	II to adjust
عُمْلة	currency
عوّض ه (من\عن)	II to reimburse (for)
عَرْض عُروض	bid, tender
غُرْفة مُحَصَّنة	strongroom
فاتورة	invoice
فائِدة فَوائِد	interest
فائِدة بَسيطة	simple interest
فائِدة مُرَكَّبة	compound interest
فائِض	surplus
قدّر (ب)	II to evaluate (at)
قَرْض قُروض	loan
قَرْض مُنْخَفِض الفائِدة	soft loan, low-interest loan
قيّد هـ (لِحِساب)	II to credit (an account) with
قيّد على هـ	II to debit s.o. with s.t.
قيّم (ب)	II to evaluate (at)
قيمة قِيَم	value
كَشْف حِساب	bank/financial statement
كلّف (ه) هـ	II to cost (s.o.) s.t.
مالي	financial
ماليّة	finance

مَبْلَغ مَبالِغ	amount
مَبْلَغ مُسْتَحَقّ	amount due
مُتَأَخِّرات	arrears
مَجْموع	total
مُحاسِب	accountant
مُحاسَبة	accounting, accountancy
رَئيس :محاسَبة المُحاسَبة	chief accountant
قِسْم المُحاسَبة:محاسَبة	accounts department
مَدين	debit, debtor
مَرْدود	yield, return
مُساهِم	shareholder
مُسْبَق	advance (adj.)
مُسْتَفيد	beneficiary
شيك مُسَطَّر :مسطر	crossed cheque
مَصْرِف مَصارِف	bank
مَصْرِفي	bank(ing) (adj.)
مُكافَأة	bonus
مَكْشوف	uncovered, overdrawn
	(amount, account etc.)
مُلْكِيّة	property
مِلْكِيّة	ownership

مُمْتَلَكات .pl	property
مَنْفَعة	benefit
مَوْجودات .pl	assets
موّل	II to finance
ميزان مَوازين	balance
ميزانيّة	budget
نِسْبة	rate
نَفَقة نِفاق\sound	expenditure
نَقْد نُقود	cash, (pl.) money
وَديعة وَدائِع	deposit
يَنّ	yen
يورو	euro

4. INSURANCE

أجّر	II to let/lease out
أُجْرة	rent
أُجْرة الأرْض	ground rent
تَأْمين ضد جَميع :أخطار الأخْطار	all-risks insurance
ادّع	VIII to claim
بأرْباح	with profits (policy etc.)
مُشاركة :أرْباح في الأرْباح	participation in profits
استأجِر	X to hold/take on lease
سِعْر\قيمة :استبدال الاسْتِبْدال	replacement cost/value
استفاد (من)	X to benefit (from)
اسْتِهْلاك عادي مَعْقول	fair wear and tear
البَلَى والتَلَف :استهلاك بالاسْتِهْلاك العادي	fair wear and tear
إصابة	injury
إصابة صِناعيّة	industrial injury
اِصْطِدام	collision
أصلح هـ\من	IV to repair

:أضرار	تَأْمين ضد الأضرار	damage insurance
	الْتِزام (بـ)	obligation, liability (for)
	أمّن	II to insure/assure
	أمّن على	II to underwrite
	أهمل	IV to neglect
	بوليصة بَوالِص	(insurance) policy
	تَأْمين	insurance/assurance
	تَأْمين بَحْري	marine insurance
	تَأْمين طبّي	medical insurance
:تأمين	قابِل للتَأْمين	insurable
:تأمين	وَثيقة تَأْمين	insurance policy
	تَصادُم	collision
	تَعاوُني	mutual (assurance, policy etc.)
	تَعْرِفة	tariff
:تعويض	قَسْم التَعْويضات	claims department
	تَعْويضات .pl	(payment for) damages
	تَعْويضي	compensatory
	تنازل (لـ) عن	III to assign (to)/waive (in favour of)
	حادِث حَوادِث	accident

	حادِث صِناعي	industrial accident
	حَريق حَرائِق	fire
حريق:	تَأُمين ضد	fire insurance
	الحَريق	
حوادث:	تَأُمين ضد	accident insurance
	الحوادث	
	حَياة حَيَوات	life
حياة:	تَأُمين على الحَياة	life assurance
حياة:	لِمَدى الحَياة	whole-life (adj.)
	خَبير حِسابات	actuary
	شـؤون التأُمين	
	خَسارة خَسائِر	damage, loss
	خَسارة كُلِّيّة	total loss
	خَطَر أَخْطار	risk
	دَفْعة سَنَويّة	annuity
	سدّد	II to settle/defray/discharge
سَرِقة:	سَرَقَ (ه\مِن) هـ	I *i* to steal (from)
سرقة:	تَأُمين ضد	theft insurance
	السَرِقة	
سفر:	تَأُمين السَفَر	travel insurance
	شامِل	comprehensive

صاحِب أصْحاب	owner (of property), holder (of policy)
ضَرَر أضْرار	damage
ضرّر	II to damage
ضَمِنَ ل هـ ضَمان	I *a* to guarantee
طارِئ	contingency
طَبيعي	natural
طَرَف ثالِث	third party
طَلَبَ طَلَب	I *u* to claim, to apply for
عَقار	(piece of) real estate, premises
تَعْويض العُمّال :عمّال	workmen's compensation
عوّض ه (من\عن)	II to compensate (for)/ indemnify (against)
تَأْمين ضد الغَيْر :غير	third-party insurance
تَأْمين ضد الفَيَضان :فيضان	flood insurance
قِسْط أقْساط	premium
كارِثة كَوارِث	disaster
مُدَّعٍ (المُدَّعي)	claimant
إهْمال مُساعِد :مساعد	contributory negligence
مُسْتَأْجِر	tenant, lessee
مَسْؤول (عن)	responsible/liable (for)

مَسْؤوليّة (عن) liability (for)

مُعَدَّل rate

بوليصة مُعَيِّنة :معّن named policy

مُكافَأَة bonus

مَلَكَ مُلْك\مِلْك I i to own

مِلْك أَمْلاك property (thing owned)

مَنْفَعة مَنافِع benefit

مؤَمَّن insured (thing)

مؤَمِّن insurer, underwriter

مؤَمَّن عليه insured (person)

ناتِج (عن) consequential (upon),

resulting (from)

نِسْبة نِسَب rate

5. LAW & CONTRACT

أبْطل	IV to annul
اتِّفاق	agreement (action/document)
اتَّفق مع على	VIII to agree with s.o. on s.t.
اتّهم (ب)	VIII to accuse (of)
أثبت	IV to prove
إجْباري	compulsory
إجْراءات	proceedings
اِحْتِيال	fraud
اِحْتِيالي	fraudulent
دائِرة :اختْصاص اخْتِصاص	jurisdiction
اختلس	VIII to embezzle
اِخْتِياري	optional
أخلّ ب	IV to infringe/violate
إخْلال بالعَقْد	breach of contract
ادَّع	VIII to allege
استأنف (هـ)	X to appeal (against)
مَحْكَمة :استئناف الاسْتِئْناف	court of appeal
استجْوَب	X to cross-examine

	اِسْمي	nominal
	أصدر	IV to pronounce
	افترى على	VIII to slander
	ألغى	IV to cancel
انسحاب:	شَرْط	escape clause
انْسِحاب		
انقضاء:	تاريخ انْقِضاء	expiry date
	انقضى	VII to expire
	إهانة المَحْكَمة	contempt of court
	أهْليّة	competence
	أهمل	IV to neglect, to fail to fulfil
	أوجب على هـ	IV to impose on s.o. s.t.
	باطِل	null, void
	بَنْد بُنود	clause, article
	تاريخ الاسْتِحْقاق	due date
	تَجَسُّس صِناعي	industrial espionage
	تَحْكيم	arbitration
	تَسْوية وَدّيّة	amicable settlement
	تَعْويض	compensation, damages
تمييز:	مَحْكَمة تَمْييز	court of appeal
	تواطأ (على)	VI to collude (in)
	توسّط لـ (بـ\بين\في)	VI to mediate for (between/in)

توقّف عن	V to suspend/discontinue, to be dependent/conditional on
تَوْكيل رَسْمي	power of attorney
جاسوسيّة صِناعيّة	industrial espionage
في حالة	in (the) case of (in cst.)
حَجَزَ هـ\على حَجْز	I u/i to impound
حَجْز (على)	distraint (of)
حَدَّ حَدَّ حُدود	I u to limit/confine
حدّد	II to define
حَقّ حُقوق (في)	right (n.) (to/of)
حَقّ التَأْليف وَالنَشْر	copyright
حَقّ حَجْز	lien
الحَقّ عليه	he is (in the) wrong
الحَقّ معه	he is (in the) right
حَقيقة حَقائِق	truth
حُكْم أَحْكام	judgement, ruling
حَكَمَ على حُكْم أَحْكام	I u to judge, give judgement on
حلّف	II to swear in
خالف	III to infringe/violate
خِلاف	dispute
دَعا	I u to summon
دَعْوة دَعاوِي\sound	case, lawsuit

	رَفَضَ رَفْض	I i to dismiss (a case)
	رَمْزي	nominal
	سابِقة	precedent
:سريان	مُدّة سَرَيان	period of validity
	سوّى	II to settle
	شَرْط شُروط	(pre-)condition, clause
(أنْ)	بِشَرْط\على شَرْط	on condition (that) or in cst.
	شَرْط خَزائي	penalty clause
	شَرْعي	valid, lawful
	شَرْعية	validity, legitimacy
:شرف	اتِّفاق شَرَف	gentlemen's agreement
	شَفَهي	verbal
	شَفَوي	oral
	شَكْلاً وموْضوعاً	in form and content/substance
	شَهادة	testimony, evidence
	شَهِدَ (ب\أنّ) شَهادة	I a to testify (to, that)
	شهّر ب	II to libel
	صادر	III to seize/confiscate
	صَحيح صِحاح	true, correct
	ضِمْني	implicit
	طَرَف أطْراف	party
	طَعَنَ على\في طَعْن	I u/a to libel

	عَادِل	equitable, fair
	عَدْل	justice
:عمل	قَانون العَمَل	labour law
:عمل	مَحْكَمة العَمَل	labour court
	عَقْد عُقود	contract
	غَرامة	fine (n.), penalty
	غرّم	II to fine
	فَاوض	III to negotiate
	فَسَخَ فَسْخ	I a to annul
	قَاضٍ (القاضي) قُضاه	judge
	قَاضى	III to sue
	قَاعة مَحْكَمة	courtroom
	قَانون قَوانين	law
	قَانوني	legal
	قُوَة قاهِرة	force majeure
	كَاذِب	false
	لاغٍ (اللاغي)	null, void
	مُحامٍ (المُحامي)	lawyer
	مَحْدود	fixed, definitive
	مَحْكَمة مَحاكِم	lawcourt
:محلّف	هَيْئة مُحَلَّفين	jury
	مُخادِع	swindler

مُخاصِم	adversary, litigant
مُدَّعٍ (المُدَّعِي)	plaintiff
مُدَّعًى (المُدَّعى) عليه	respondent, defendant
مَدَني	civil (law, case)
مَشْروط	conditional
مُصادَرة	seizure, confiscation
مَصاريف	costs
مُعَيَّن	definite, specific
مُقاضاة	litigation
مَقْصود	intentional
مُلْحَق	appendix, rider
مُلْزِم (على)	binding (upon)
مِلْك أَمْلاك	estate
قابِل لِلمُناقَشة :مناقشة	negotiable
مُؤَهَّل	competent
نازع ه هـ	III to dispute s.t. with s.o.
نَصَحَ (ل ب)	I a to advise (s.o. on s.t.)
نفّذ	to fulfil/execute/enforce
وَحيد	exclusive
وَكالة رَسْمِيّة	power of attorney

6. RESEARCH & PRODUCTION

	أجْهِزة .pl	equipment
	اِخْتِبار	experiment
	اِخْتِباري	experimental
	اختبر	VIII to test
	استبدل (هـ ب)	X to replace (s.t. with s.t.)
	آلة	device, machine, instrument
	آلي	mechanical
	أمان	safety
	إنْتاج	production
:إنْتاج	مَحَطّة إنْتاج	production station
	إنْتاجيّة	productivity
:إنْتاجية تَحْسين الإنْتاجيّة	اِتّفاقيّة	productivity agreement
:إنْتاجية تَحْسين الإنْتاجيّة	حَمْلة	productivity drive/campaign
:إنْتاجية تَحْسين الإنْتاجيّة	مُفاوَضة	productivity bargaining
	أنتج	IV to produce
	انفجر .int	VII to explode
:أوّلي	مادّة أوّليّة	raw material

	بِتْرَوْل	petroleum
	بَحَثَ (هـ\عن) بَحْث	I *a* to do research (in)
	بَحْث أَبْحاث	research
	البَحْث والتَنْمِية	research and development
	بَطّارِيّة	battery
	بْلاسْتيك	plastic (n.)
	بِناء	construction
	بِنائي	construction (adj.)
	بِئْر آبار .f	well (n.)
	تَجْرِبة تَجارِب	test, experiment
	تَجْريب	test, trial
	تَجْريبي	experimental
:تجميع	خَطّ تَجْميع	assembly line
	تخصّص (ل\ب\في)	V to specialise (in)
:تكرير	مَحَطّة تَكْرير	refinery
	جدّد	II to renew/renovate/ modernise
	جرّب هـ	II to test, to experiment with
	جمّع	II to assemble (parts)
:جملة	إنْتاج بِالجُمْلة	mass production
	جِهاز أَجْهِزة	device, set
	جِيَوْلَوْجي	geological, geologist

	حدَّث	II to modernise
	حَديد	iron (n.)
	حَفَّار	driller
	حَفَرَ حَفْر	I i to drill
حفر:	جِهاز حَفْر	drilling rig
خام:	زَيْت\نَفْط خام	crude oil
	خَرْج	output
	دائِرة دَوائِر	circuit
	دَرَجة	degree
	دَرَجة حَرارة	temperature
	ركَّب	II to install
	زُجاج	glass (n.)
	زَيْت زُيوت	oil
	زيَّت	II to lubricate
	سَلامة	safety
سلامة:	مَسْؤُول سَلامة	safety officer
	سَماد أسْمِدة	fertiliser
	شحَّم	II to lubricate
	شَحَنَ (ب) شَحْن	I a to charge (battery), to load (with)
	شغَّل هـ	II to operate s.t.
	صانَ صِيانة	I ū to maintain

صلّح	II to repair
صمّم	II to design
صِناعي	synthetic, artificial
صَنَعَ صَنْع\صُنْع	I *a* to manufacture
صَهْريج صَهاريج	tank (vessel for gas or liquid)
صِيانة	maintenance
طاقة	energy
عاطِل	idle (machinery)
عالِم عُلَماء	scientist
عِلْمي	scientific
عَمَليّة	operation, process
عَيْب عُيوب	defect
غاز	gas
قِطْعة غَيار :غِيار	spare part
فَنّي	technical, technician
فولاذ	steel (n.)
قاسَ قَيْس\قِياس	I *i* to measure
قِطْعة قِطَع	part, component
كرّر	II to refine
كَسْر كُسور	fraction (of crude oil)
كَهْرَبا\كَهْرَباء	electricity
اِخْتِصاصي :كهرباء	electrician

بالكَهْرَباء	
كَهْرَبائي	electric(al)
كيمياء	chemistry
كيميائي	chemical, chemist
مادّة مَوادّ	material (n.)
مُحَرِّك	engine
مُحَلِّل	analyst
مُخْتَبَر	laboratory
مُراقَبة كَمِّيّة	quantity control
مُراقَبة نَوْعيّة	quality control
مَرْفَق مَرافِق	utility (electricity, gas etc.)
مَشْغَل مَشاغِل	workshop
مَصْنَع مَصانِع	factory
مِضَجّة	pump
مُعَطَّل	idle (machinery)
مَعْمَل مَعامِل	laboratory
مُنْتَج	product
مُنْتِج	productive, producer
مُهَنْدِس	engineer
مُوَلِّد	generator
ميكانيك	mechanics
ميكانيكي	mechanic, mechanical

	celsius	مِئَوي
	defective	ناقِص
	oil	نَفْط
	shift	نَوْبة نُوَب
	engineering	هَنْدَسة
:وقت	time and motion study	دِراسة الوَقْت والحَرَكة
	fuel	وُقود

7. PUBLICITY & MARKETING

اتِّجاه	trend
اخْتِيار	choice
إخْلاص لِلمارْكة	brand loyalty
اسْتَغَلّ ه هـ	X to exploit (fairly or unfairly)
اسْتِغْلالي	profiteer(ing)
اسْتِمارة الطَلَب	order form
اسْتِهْلاكي	consumer (adj.)
استهلك	X to consume
قائِمة أسْعار :أسعار	price list
مُراقَبة أسْعار :أسعار	price control
اشتری	VIII to buy
إعْلان	advertisement/advertising (n.)
وَسائِل إعْلان :إعلان	advertising media
أعلن	IV to advertise
أغرق	IV to dump (sell at low price)
مَتْجَر (ذو) أقْسام :أقسام	department store
باعَ بَيْع\مَبيع	I ī to sell
بائِع باعة	salesman
بائِعة	saleswoman
إعْلان جَماعي :بريد	mail shot

	بِالبَريد	
طلَب بَريدي\ :بريد(ي)		mail order
	بِالبَريد	
	بَيْع	sale
	لِلبَيْع	for/on sale
	لِلبَيْع أوْ لِلرَدّ	on sale or return
:بيع	آلة بَيْع	vending machine
	تاجر ه ب\في	III to trade (with s.o. in s.t.)
:تجارة	مَحَلّ تِجارة	trade outlet
:تجاري	سُمْعة تِجاريّة	goodwill
	تَرْويج	promotion, merchandising
:تسويق	شَرِكة تَسْويق	marketing company
	تَصْريف	merchandising (n.)
	تَصْفِية	clearance (sale)
	تَفْضيلي	preferential
:تقسيط	شِراء	hire-purchase
	بِالتَقْسيط	
	تَنافُسي	competitive
	تَكْلفة تَكاليف	cost
:توزيع	تَسَلْسُل التَوْزيع	distribution chain
	جارٍ (الجاري)	going (rate, price etc.)
	جُمْلة	wholesale (n.)

بِالجُمْلة	wholesale (adj./adverb)
حَدّي	marginal
حَمْلة حَمَلات	campaign, drive
خِدْمة زَبائِن	customer service
خَصْم	discount
خفَّض هـ	II to reduce s.t.
دِراسة السوق	market research/study
دِعايَة	publicity, advertising
رَخيص	cheap, inexpensive
روَّج	II to promote
زائِد	excess/surplus (adj.)
زَبون زَبائِن	customer
ساوم ه\ب في\على	III to bargain (with s.o. over s.t.)
سائِد	going (rate, price etc.)
سِجِلّ الطَلَبات التِجاريّة	order book
سعَّر	II to price
سِعْر أسْعار	price
سِعْر الطَلَب	asking price
سِعْر مَعْروض	offer price
سِلْعة سِلَع	commodity
سوق أسْواق f.	market

سوّق	II to market
شِراء	purchasing
شُهْرة	goodwill
صاحِب اِمْتِياز	concessionaire, franchise holder
صادِرات	exports
صدّر	II to export
طلَبَ مِن هـ طلَب	I *u* to demand/order (goods)
طلَب	demand/order (of goods)
عند الطلَب	on demand/request
عَرَضَ هـ عَرْض	I *i* to exhibit
عَرَضَ على هـ عَرْض	I *i* to offer
العَرْض والطلَب	supply and demand
عَلامة تِجاريّة	trade mark
وَلاء لَلعَلامة التِجاريّة :علامة	brand loyalty
غالٍ (الغالي)	expensive
فَصْلي	seasonal
قُوّة شِرائيّة	purchasing power
قُوَى السوق	market forces
كاتالوج	(*katalūg*) catalogue
كلَّف (ه) هـ	II to cost (s.o.) s.t.

luxury	كَمالي	
luxury goods	سِلَع كَمالِيَّة	كمالي:
brand	مارْكة	
sale	مَبيع	
sales turnover	رَقْم المَبيعات	مبيع:
gross sales, sales turnover	مَبيعات إجْمالِيّة .pl	
shop, store	مَتْجَر مَتاجِر	
durable	مَتين	
reduced	مُخَفَّض	
high, rising, raised	مُرْتَفِع	
auction	مَزاد	
second-hand	مُسْتَعْمَل	
consumer (n.)	مُسْتَهْلِك	
buyer	مُشْتَرٍ (المُشْتَري)	
purchase	مُشْتَرًى (المُشْتَرى)	
purchasing (n.)	مُشْتَرَيات .pl	
exhibition	مَعْرِض مَعارِض	
exhibit(s)	مَعْروضات .pl	
retail (adj./adverb)	بالمُفَرَّق	
representative	ممثِّل	
low	مُنْخَفِض	
door-to-door (adj.)	مَنْزِلي	

عند المُوافَقة	on approval
مَوْسِمي	seasonal
مُؤَلِّف إعْلانات	(advertising) copywriter
نُقْطة البَيْع	point of sale
نَموذَج طَلَب	order form
وزّع	II to distribute

8. STORAGE, TRANSPORT & TRAVEL

أبْحر	IV to set sail (of a ship)
إجْراءات	formalities (customs etc.)
أُجْرة	fare, freight charge
إرْسال	despatch
أرسل	IV to send
استأجر	X to charter
استورد	X to import
أُسْطول أساطيل	fleet (ships or aircraft)
إعْلان	declaration (customs etc.)
أقْلع	IV to take off (of an aircraft)
انتظار: قاعة انْتِظار	waiting-room
انْتِقال	relocation, transition
أودع ه هـ	IV to consign/entrust to s.o. s.t.
بَحْري	sea (adj.)
بَرّي	land (adj.)
برّي: نَقْل بَرّي	road haulage
بَضائع مودَعة بإشْراف الجُمْرُك\الحُكومة	bonded goods
بَعَثَ (ه) هـ\ب بَعْث	I a to send s.t. (to s.o.)

	بوليصة شَحْن	bill of lading
	بَيان	declaration (customs etc.)
	تَأْشيرة	visa
	تَخْزين	storage
	تَذْكَرة تَذاكِر	ticket
	تَفْتيش تَفاتيش	inspection
	تَكْديس	stacking
: تلف	سَريع التَلَف	perishable
	توجّه إلى	V to head for
	جَرَدَ هـ جَرْد	I u to make an inventory/
		take stock of
	جُمْرُك جَمارِك	customs
	جَواز سَفَر	passport
	جَوّي	air (adj.)
:حاجة	زائِد عن الحاجة	surplus to requirements
	حاوية	container
	حَجْم حُجوم	volume, bulk
	حَمَلَ حَمْل	I i to carry/convey
	حُمولة	cargo
	حَوْض السُفُن	dock
	خُروج	exit (action)
	خَزَن خَزْن	I u to store/stock

	دُخول	entry (action)
ذَهاب:	تَذْكَرة ذَهاب وَإياب	return ticket
	رافِعة	crane
	راكِب رُكّاب	passenger
	رُبّان رُبّانيّة	(ship's) captain
	رِحْلة	trip, journey
	رَسْم رُسوم	duty, tax, fee
	رَسَى int.	I ī to berth/dock
	رَصيف أَرْصِفة	wharf, quay, pier, platform
	رَكِبَ هـ رُكوب	I a to get in/on (a means of transport)
	زارَ زِيارة	I u to visit
	زائِد	excess (adj.), excessive
	زائِر زُوّار	visitor
	سافَر	III to travel
	ساقَ سِياقة	I ū to drive
	سائِب	bulk (adj.)
	سائِق	driver
	سَفَر	journey
	سَفينة سُفُن	ship
	سِكّة (pl. سِكَك) حَديديّة	railway

سيف   c. i. f. (cost, insurance and freight)

شاحنة   truck, lorry

شَحَنَ (هـ) بِ شَحْن   I *a* to load (a carrier) with s.t.

شَحَنَ هـ شَحْن   I *a* to load (goods)

شَحْن   load, cargo, freight

شحن: وَثيقة شَحْن جوّي   air waybill

شَحْنة شَحَنات   lading, consignment

صادرات   exports

صدّر   II to export

ضخم: ناقلة ضَخْمة   supertanker

طارَ طَيَران   I *i* to fly

طائرة   aircraft

طَريق طُرُق m./f.   road

عن طَريق   via, by way of

طُنّ أطْنان   ton(ne)

طَيّار   (aircraft) pilot

طَيَران   flight

غادر هـ   III to leave, to depart from

فتّش   II to inspect

فرّغ هـ   to unload (a cargo)

فوب	f. o. b. (free on board)
قادَ قيادة	I *ū* to drive
قِطار	train
كَدَسَ هـ كَدْس	I *i* to stack
كدّس هـ	II to stack
مِتْر أمْتار	metre
على مَتْن	on board (also in cst.)
مُحْتَوَيات	contents
مَحَطّة	station
مَخْزَن مَخازِن	store(room)
مَخْزَن إيداع بِإشْراف الجُمْرُك\الحُكومة	bonded warehouse
مَخْزون	stock
مَدْفوع النَقْل	carriage paid
مِتْر مُرَبَّع مربّع:	square metre
مُرْسَل	consigned, deposited
مُرْسِل	consignor, depositor
مُرْسَل إليه	consignee, depository
مَرْسًى (المَرْسى) مَراسٍ (المَراسي)	anchorage, berth, mooring
مُرْشِد	(ship's) pilot
مَرْكَب مَراكِب	vessel

	مُرور	transit
	مُسَبَّق	advance (adj.)
	مُسْتَوْدَع	depot, warehouse
	مُسْتَوْرَدات	imports
	مَطار	airport
مكعّب:	مِتْر مُكعَّب	cubic metre
	مِلاحة	shipping, navigation
	مُلْحَق تِجاري	commercial attaché
مِنشأ:	شَهادة مَنْشأ	certificate of origin
	مِنْطَقة حُرّة	free zone
m./f. \ مَواني‌ء	ميناء	port
مَوانٍ (المَواني)		
	ميناء حُرّ(ة)	free port
	ناقِل	carrier (vessel, vehicle)
	ناقِلة بِتْرَوْل	tanker
	نَزَلَ نُزول	I *i* to land (of an aircraft)
	نُزول	landing, stopover
	نَقْل	transport
	هِجَرة	immigration
	وارِدات	imports
	وَصَلَ (إلى) وُصول	I *i* to arrive (at)

9. PERSONNEL

أَبَوي	paternalist(ic)
إجازة	leave
إجازة مَرَضيّة	sick leave
أجْر أجور	wage
إجْراءات شَكْوى	grievance procedure
إدارة شُؤُون المُوَظَّفين	personnel administration
استحقّ	X to merit
استخدم	X to recruit/employ
اسْتِشار	consultation
استقال (عن\من)	X to resign (from)
أضرب	IV to strike
إعادة التَوْظيف	reinstatement
أقْدَميّة	seniority
إنْذار	warning, warning letter
بَدَل أبْدال\sound	allowance
بَطالة	unemployment
تَأْديبي	disciplinary
تَحْكيم	arbitration
تَدْريب	training
تَدْريب أثناء\على	on-the-job training

العَمَل

تَسْريح	dismissal
تَعْويض	compensation
تَغَيُّب	absenteeism
تقاعد	VI to retire
تَقْدير المُوَظَّفين	staff appraisal
تَقْييم الوَظيفة	job evaluation
تَمْييز (ضد)	discrimination (against)
تَنْفيذي	executive (adj.)
مُدير تَنْفيذي :تنفيذي	line manager
وَكالة تَوْظيف :توظيف	employment agency/bureau
جَدْوَل الرَواتِب	pay scale
حادِث حَوادِث	accident
حَرَكيّة	mobility (workforce, jobs etc.)
حَكَم حُكّام	referee
خِبْرة	experience
خِدْمة	service
دَرَجة	grade
رابط int III	to picket
راتِب رَواتِب	salary
راتِب صافٍ	nett salary, take-home pay
راقب III	to supervise

رُتْبة رُتَب	grade
رُخْصة عَمَل	work permit
رَفاهيّة	welfare
رقّى	II to promote
رَمْزي	token (payment, strike etc.)
رَواتِب مُتَساوِية	equal pay
زائِد عن الحاجة	redundant
زيادة عن الحاجة	redundancy
ساوم (ه على\في)	III to bargain (with over)
سُلَّم رَواتِب	salary range
شُغْل إضافي	overtime (work)
شَكْوَى شكاوى	complaint, grievance
شَهادة شَخْصيّة	(candidate's) reference
صاحِب العَمَل	employer
الضَمان الاجْتِماعي	social security
طَلَب	application, request
ظُروف العَمَل	working conditions
عاطِل (عن العَمَل)	unemployed
عامِل عُمّال	workman
عَزَلَ (عن) عَزْل	I i to dismiss (from)
عَلاقات صِناعيّة	industrial relations
عِلاوَة	increment

عُنْصُريّة	racism
عيّن ه (ه)	II to appoint (as)
فاوض ه\مع هـ	III to negotiate
فائِدة إضافيّة	fringe benefit
فَحْص طِبّي	medical examination
قُوّة عامِلة	manpower
كاتِب كُتّاب	(male) clerk
كاتِبة	(female) clerk
مُوَظَّف كِتابي :كِتابي	clerk
كَفاءة	qualification
ماهِر	skilled
راتِب مُتَأَخِّر :متأخر	back pay
غير مُتَفَرِّغ :متفرغ	part-time
مُتَقاعِد	pensioner
مَحْسوبيّة	nepotism
مُراقِب	supervisor, foreman
مُرَشَّح	candidate
بَرْنامَج عَمَل مَرِن :مرن	flexible working
مُساوَمة جَماعيّة	collective bargaining
مُسْتَخْدِم	employer
مُشْرِف	supervisor
مُصالَحة	conciliation

expense account	حِساب	مصروف:
	مَصْروفات	
(retirement) pension	مَعاش (تَقاعُد)	
cost of living	تَكاليف	معيشة:
	المَعيشة	
expatriate	مُغْتَرِب	
closed shop	مَشْغَل مُقْفَل	مقفل:
interview	مُقابَلة	
remuneration	مُكافأة	
shop steward	مُمَثِّل النقابة	
dispute	مُنازَعة	
shift	مُناوَبة	
shop steward	مَنْدوب (العُمّال)	
vacancy	مَنْصِب شاغِر	
career, profession	مِهْنة مِهَن	
employee	مُوَظَّف	
executive (n.)	مُوَظَّف تَنْفيذي	
junior staff employee	مُوَظَّف صَغير	
senior staff employee	مُوَظَّف كَبير	
qualified, skilled	مُؤَهَّل	
qualification (for a job)	مُؤَهِّل	
psychology	عِلْم النفْس	نفس:

نَفْسي	psychological
نَقابة عُمّال	trade union
نَموذَج طَلَب	application form
نيابة	deputyship
نيابةً عن	acting for
وِزارة العَمَل	Ministry of Labour
وَزير العَمَل	Minister of Labour
وَصْف وَظيفة	job description
وَظائِف خالِية	situations vacant
وَظائِف مَطْلوبة	situations wanted
وَظّف	II to recruit
وَظيفة وَظائِف	job, post
وَظيفة: بـِحُكْم الوَظيفة	ex-officio

10. MEETINGS & CONFERENCES

اتّخذ	VIII to adopt
اجتمع	VIII to have a meeting
بالاجْماع\اجْماعي	unanimous (vote etc.)
أجمع (على)	IV to be unanimous (on)
احتجّ (على)	VIII to protest (against)
اختصر	VIII to summarise
أرجأ	IV to adjourn/suspend
إرْشادات	guidelines
تَعْليمات :إرشادي	guidelines
إرْشاديّة	
استأنف هـ	X to resume
استنتج (من)	X to deduce/infer (from)
اشترك في	VIII to participate in
اعتذر عن الغياب	VIII to apologise for absence
اعترض (على)	VIII to object (to)
أعطى ه الكَلمة	IV to give the floor to
إعْلان	announcement, communiqué
أيّة أعْمال أُخْرى :أعمال	any other business
افْتتاحي	inaugural
اقْتراح بالشُكْر	vote of thanks

اقترح	VIII to move/propose
اقترع (على)	VIII to ballot (on)
ألقى	IV to deliver (speech etc.)
امتنع (عن)	VIII to abstain (from)
انتخب	VIII to co-opt/elect
انتقد هـ\على	VIII to find fault with
أوجز	IV to summarise
ائتمر	VIII to confer
أيّد	II to support/second/endorse
بالغ في	III to exaggerate/overstate
بَحَثَ هـ بَحْث بُحوث	I a to discuss
بَعْثة بَعَثات	mission, delegation
بِناءً على	on the basis of
بَنّاء	constructive (idea etc.)
بَيان صُحُفي	press release
تَبادُل الآراء	exchange of views
تبنّى	V to adopt (resolution etc.)
تذكّر	V to remember/bear in mind
ترأّس	V to be appointed chairman
ترجم تَرْجَمة	IQ to translate
ترجم شَفَهيًا	IQ to interpret
تَرْجَمة مُتَزامَنة	simultaneous translation

تَصْويت على\بِالثِقة	vote of confidence
تَوْجيهي	guiding (principles etc.)
جَدْوَل أعْمال	agenda
جَلْسة	session
حاسِم	conclusive
خِطاب	speech, address
داوِل هـ III	to circulate
دَعا ه هـ دُعاء I ū	to convene
دَعا ه هـ ثانيةً I ū	to reconvene
دوّن II	to note
ذَكَرَ ذِكْر I u	to mention
ذكّر ه ب II	to remind s.o. of s.t.
راجِع هـ III	to review/reiterate,
	to revert to
رأسَ هـ رِئاسة\رِياسة I a	to preside over, to chair
رَأْي آراء	opinion
رحّب ب II	to welcome
رَئيس رُؤَساء	chairman
سانِد III	to support
ساوِم (ه) III	to bargain (with)
سجّل II	to place on record
سلّم ب II	to concede

صدّق على II to approve

صرّح II to declare

صوّت (على\لِصالِح\ ضد) II to vote (on/for/against)

ضِمْني tacit

طَلَبَ فُرْصة الكَلام I u to ask for the floor

عَرَضَ للبَحْث I i to table

عَقَدَ عَقْد I u to hold (conference etc.)

عُنْوان عَناوين heading, title

غابَ (عن) غِياب I ī to be absent (from)

غَيْر عادي extraordinary (meeting etc.)

فاوض III to negotiate

قاطع III to interrupt

قَرار resolution

الكَلِمة مع ... ... has the floor

لَجْنة دائِمة standing committee

لَجْنة فَرْعِيّة sub-committee

مُتَحَدِّث speaker (person speaking)

مُتَحَدِّث باسْم spokesman for (in cst.)

مُحادَثات talks

مُحاضَرة talk, lecture, address

مَحْضَر الاِجْتِماع minutes

مُطْلَق	absolute (majority etc.)
مُقَدَّمة	premise
مُكْتَمِل	plenary
مَنْدوب	delegate
مُؤْتَمَر	conference
مُؤَجَّل	deferred
ناطِق بِلِسان	spokesman
نائِب نُوّاب	representative, delegate
نِصاب	quorum
نِطاق البَحْث	terms of reference
نَفى نَفْي	I *ī* to deny, repudiate
نَقَدَ نَقْد	I *u* to examine critically
نَقَدَ بِسَبَب	I *u* to criticise for
نُقْطة نِظاميّة	point of order
وَثيقة وَثائِق	document
وُجْهة نَظَر	point of view
وصّى ه ب	II to recommend
وَفْد وُفُود	delegation
وَفْقًا ل	in accordance with

ENGLISH INDEX

The numbers refer to pages. An asterisk * following the number shows that the entry appears more than once on that page. The sign ~ repeats the headword (or that part of it preceding the hyphen). The sign ≈ repeats the headword (or that part of it preceding the hyphen) but with a capital initial letter. Abbreviated titles such as IMF are not listed; search under the first word of the full title.